WINDOWS 10

USER MANUAL

FOR **SENIORS**

**Comprehensive Guide to Exploring
Windows 10 Tricks, Shortcuts &
Troubleshooting**

Stephen W. Rock

Dedicated to all my readers

Acknowledgement

Ii want to say a very big thank you to Michael Lime, a 3D builder, my colleague. He gave me moral support throughout the process of writing this book.

Table of Contents

Introduction

The title of this book already gives a hint on what the book is about. It is a guide for new users of any of the Windows 10 operating system.

Readers will be introduced into Windows 10 proper, learn Windows 10 networking basics and be taught through basic Windows 10 troubleshooting. .

Also, readers will learn how to configure and customize Windows 10, manage files and folders, and then handle Windows 10 settings.

The last chapters discusses tips and tricks for Windows 10; including basic tips for using Cortana, the voice assistant. .

Now, start savoring the content of this book.

Chapter 1

What is Windows 10

Windows 10 is an operating system for personal computers made by Microsoft. The Windows 10, released on July 2015 is said to be the successor of Windows 8. We all know that when it comes to operating system for personal computers, Microsoft has been taking the lead, for decades in fact.

With the Windows 10, Microsoft released **universal apps**. These are apps that are made to be used on PC, gaming consoles, smartphones, tablets, X box One and so on. The Windows 10 has some abilities that are built in to it. This a makes the IT section be able to use MDM software to control and safeguard gadgets that are running the windows 10

One feature of the windows 10 is the famous start menu, this menu was formerly just a list of programs but with the windows 10, you get live tiles appear when you hit the start.

Also with the Windows 10 Continuum, users are able to switch from either keyboard interface or touch screen interface, as long as the device can give both. This notices a keyboard and adjusts it to match.

With windows 10, we have the new **Microsoft Edge**. This Microsoft Edge becomes the default web browser taking the place of internet explorer. With Microsoft Edge we have new tools like Web **Notes** and **Reading view**.

With Web Notes, users have the power to mark-up the websites that they visit. And you know how ads makes reading websites difficult and all choked up, you don't find that with Windows 10. Reading View enables users the power to go through websites without the disturbance of ads.

Edge also comes with Cortana. Cortana is the digital assistant of Microsoft. This assistant is embedded into the new operating system and it is synced together with Bing. This supports voice input and text for command.

It analyzes email, texts, communication history, browsing history and apps so that it can tailor the Windows 10 to give you the best experience you can get. If you know your stuff with IT, you can disable Cortana. Just got to **Group Policy Settings** and do your thing.

With the previous operating system, Windows 8, Microsoft tried to make the user interface go well for tablets and smartphones. But with PCs, it's does not form a good relationship. But with Windows 10, Microsoft did a lot better and they addressed other problems and obstacle they faced with windows 8.

Normal users and even IT professionals, think of Windows 10 to be a lot more enterprise-friendly than the previous OS. This is because of the friendly desktop layout that resembles the Windows 7. Cortana has also helped this new OS gain more support.

Chapter 2

How To Install Windows 10

So you're tired of your old windows. Or maybe you just want to be up to date with the newer trend. It time you switch to windows 10 the newest Operating System from Microsoft.

But installing can be kind of tricky and you might not know what to do. Here are steps to upgrade to windows 10.

Entering the Installer for Windows 10

1. If you want to install Windows 10 on your computer, you should make sure that you have the windows installation file put into a flash drive or a disc already. If by chance you haven't downloaded the installation tool for Windows 10, head over to www.microsoft.com.

2. Now that you have that sorted, insert the disc or flash into your computer

3. Press the Windows key on the keyboard or you can just click the Windows symbol and the left corner of the screen

4. Select Power and a list should show up, click **Restart**

5. On startup, your computer should show a message that says you should press a key to go to setup. Look out for that message or something like that as you computer restarts. Press whatever key it tells you to, in most cases, it's the F2 key.

6. In the setup, Use the arrow keys to find your way and navigate to the **Boot**. Click it. IF you see **Boot options** and not **Boot**, still click it. It the same thing.

7. From here you will see a list of different device that it should boot. From the options, choose the option for CD-ROM Drive if you're using a disc to install. If your using a flash drive, choose Removable Devices

8. Hit the + plus key till your choice is at the top. For other computers you may have

press F5 or some other function key. Whether you chose CD-ROM or Removable Devices, once your choice is at the top of the option, the computer will use your selection.

9. To save what you've set, you should see prompt at the base of the screen telling you which key to press to Save. Could be F10. Once you press it, your computer will save it and restart. After it has restarted, it is time to begin the next phase.

Installing the Windows

1. The Windows Setup page should show up now. Select your desired language and hit **Next**

2. After that, a box titled **Install now** should appear. Click it.

3. You will now be asked to input you Windows 10 key. Just select **Skip** If you don't have a windows 10 key.

4. You've come this far. Don't spoil it, just tick **I accept licence terms**. Now hit **Next**

5. This step is crucial. You be asked which type of installation you want. Don't make the mistake of selecting clean install or you should just get ready to say goodbye to all your apps Settings, files. It'll be like you just got a new computer. Choose **Upgrade** instead.

6. Hope you're the patient kind, cos you're in for a real waiting stretch. You will see the window telling you it's installing Windows. This can range from an hour or more. It depends on the speed of your computer. And yeah. If you're asked to press a key so that it should boot from CD, **Don't press it. Don't**

7. Now Windows has been installed. You have the option of change the language, region, keyboard layout. Hit **Next** and you be taken to the desktop. Voila.

Chapter 3

Configuring And Customizing Windows

Using your windows normally can be nice. But adding a few tweaks and customization can take your user experience from nice to extreme delight that knows no bounds. And if you're using the latest windows, you're in for a treat as Windows 10 comes with a ton of customization options. Let's get to them, shall we?

For taking notes:

Changing The Background

This one's my favourite. It makes your computer stand out as unique. You can choose from an array of different images.

To change it,
1. Go to **Settings**
2. Select **Personalization**
3. Hit **Background**
4. There's a dropdown from **Background**, Select **picture**
5. If you choose browse, you'll be able to select an image
6. Below **Browse** you see the section Choose a fit. Form here you can select Span, Fill Center or Stretch, it's up to you.

If you love the slideshow option and want to show different pictures, just,
1. Enter **Settings**
2. Choose **Personalization**
3. Select **Background**
4. From the dropdown of **Background**, choose **Slideshow**
5. Hit **Browse** to choose a folder that contains the pictures

6. From the **Change picture every** option, select how long before a picture replaces another

Customizing The Lock Screen

With windows 10 you have the possibility of change the lock screen of the an image of your choice. To personalize and customize the lock screen,

1. Go to **Settings**
2. Select **Personalization**
3. Choose **Lock screen**
4. From the **Background** dropdown, Choose **Picture**.
5. Select **Browse** to pick an image you want to use.

Personalizing The Start Menu

The start menu is the place where you access your files, apps and other important Settings. And you also have the ability to customize it to suit your taste.

1. Go to **Settings**
2. Select **Personalization**
3. Choose **Start**. Form here you see a variety of option to change.
   - Show most used apps
   - Show more tiles on start
   - Use start full screen

   And a list of others

Changing The Color Accent

With Windows 10, you can alter the color that appears in start, title bars, taskbars and so on. If you don't really fancy the color it has now, just

1. Go to **Settings**.
2. Select **Personalization**
3. Choose **colors**
4. You have a variety of colors you can choose from, select the one that fits your taste.

Applying a Theme

Talking about themes, themes are like packages they have many images for background. They also feature sounds and color accents.

To apply a theme,
1. Enter **Settings**
2. Choose **Personalization**
3. Select **Themes**
4. Hit **Get more themes in the Store**
5. You'll be directed to the store to select the theme you desire

Chapter 4

Installing Devices

With Windows 10, you have a lot of drivers software that lets Windows access what you plug to your computer. What is supposed to happen by default is that Windows will recognize what you plug. But sometimes it starts to go to the internet to work.

During the times when you plug a gadget and Windows doesn't remember it, what you have to do is to install a Windows driver for it. What a driver should do is come with an installation program that makes everything easier and it just solves the problem. But some drivers just leave the hard stuff for you to do.

These are steps to follow if Windows doesn't recognize a plugged hardware.

1. Go to the website of the producer to get the latest driver for Windows. If you don't know their website. Just go to the life saver; Google. If you're in the website, try

looking for it in the Customer service or support area

2. Click the file you've just downloaded and it should install. After it is installed, you might find a zipper on the file, right click it.

3. Select **extract all** so you will be able to unzip it to a folder

4. If you click the downloaded file and it does not install, right click the start icon and from the menu and select **Device manager**. Once Device manger shows up, it will list out every part that is attached to or inside your PC. You should see the yellow exclamation

5. Choose the device giving problem in the Device manager and from the device mangers menu bar, select **Action**

6. Form the dropdown menu, select **Add Legacy Hardware**. This will direct you to install your hardware or your driver. This method isn't easy, even tech pros get frustrated

The only reason why you even need to install drivers is because

1. The new hardware you just bought is not working correctly. The driver is probably old Just go to the website and download.

2. You just plugged a hardware that is not recognized by Windows. If you install the latest driver, the issue should be resolved

Chapter 5

Windows Apps

Dropbox
You don't have to use OneDrive, you can use Dropbox instead. If it's your first time, you get a free 2GB storage.

Wunderlist
Wunderlist is superb for making lists, planning your stuffs or collaborating. You can setup reminders and it makes you work with them

Microsoft Stick Notes
This app allows you to create sticky notes to set reminders, digitally of course. You are able to fix on the desktop screen.

Fused
Fused is an amazing app that gives you amazing effects to your photos. Effects that normal apps don't offer. Have a look at Fused and learn how to use it effects to make your photos awesome before you upload on instagram.

VLC for Windows

VLC is a first choice for many when it comes to videos. It is well known for being able to play almost any video format. There's an updated one for Windows 10. Check it out

Adobe Photoshop Express
This allows you to have access to the photo-editing tools of Photoshop. With will make your be able to customize you images really well.

Netflix
Who doesn't know the power of Netflix. You can download it on your computer and start watching something

Duolingo
This useful app enables you be able to sharpen your kill at speaking foreign languages

Fresh Paint.
As the name suggests, this allows you to painting from a broad selection of palettes to make amazing designs

Wikipedia
With this you can search for anything in a many languages in any style you want.

Chapter 6

File And Folder Management In Windows 10

It's a given, when you're using your computer, you have to store information and the Window 10 helps you to store it. It may be music, videos or important documents. But none of this storing would have been arranged so neatly without the help of File Explorer.

Previously know as File manager then Windows explorer, File Explorer is an application on the Windows 10 that gives a nice interface for users to be able to access the files on the computer.

This File Explorer makes it easy to access files. Like for example, There's a new part titled, Quick Access. This shows up the folders and files that are recently used. This is a life saver as you might want to go to a file you open yesterday, with this new tool you don't have to go digging through your computer.

There are some tips you have to know too make your usage of file explorer the smoothest it can be.

Turn Off Or On The Ribbon

With File explorer, there is a display at the top that full and choked with commands and actions for Share, Home or View. To display the ribbon, all you have to do is to just click the tab. The ribbon should show up, this is really useful because the ribbon will come up only when you tell it to.

But if you're one that wants to see the ribbon always, all you just do is

1. Select the **Customize Quick Access Toolbar** that's at the top of the window
2. Click the **Minimize Ribbon**
3. It should remove the checkmark to show it is disabled and ribbon will display always.

Personalize The Quick Access

As we just said earlier, The Quick Access view is the part that shows up the recently used and most used files. And you can even the edit view to suit your taste.

It's not only the frequently used folder that can be in the Quick Access view. You can add other folders. To be able to do this

1. Right click on the folder you want to add to the view
2. Select **Pin to Quick Access** from the pop up
3. You should see a folder appear in the left pane of the Quick Access

Also if there's a folder you don't use very much and it's in the Quick Access view. All you do is
1. Go to the folder and right click it
2. Select **Unpin from Quick Access**

Hide Or Show The Extension Of File

File extension is method in which we identify the file type, whether it's a .jpg or .png or an audio with .wav or word document with .docx. These extensions help us know the kind of file it is. But not all find this useful.

To enable or disable this all you do is,
1. Enter the **File Explorer**
2. Click the Tab titled **View**
3. You should see **File Extensions**
4. Click the box beside it to enable
5. Click the checkmark beside it to hide extensions

Using File Explorer To Manage Images

You can use File Explorer to make some changes to your images and photos. Like for example, you don't like the orientation that an image is in, you can use File explorer to rotate.

1. Right click on the image
2. Choose either **Rotate Left** or **Rotate Right** from the menu that appears

You can also view a slideshow of photos. Make sure that the photos you want to see are all in one folder.

1. Go to **File Explorer**
2. Click the tab titled **Manage**
3. From the options on the ribbon, select the icon for **Slideshow**

All you have to do now is just sit and relax as the photos play on the screen

Or let's say you want to make a certain image the wallpaper for your desktop, all you do is right click again and choose **Set as wallpaper**.

Search For Files

With file explorer in Windows 10 you have the opportunity of searching for files or documents by their extensions or name.

1. Click the folder that the document you want to find is in
2. Check the right corner at the top to see the search area
3. Type out the name of the document or part of the name you can remember.
4. If it's a word document, you can add .doc as it's extension in the search

Chapter 7

Windows 10 Settings

As a newcomer, there are settings you must get acquainted with on your Windows 10 operating device. Do not fret; they are easy-to-do settings. Let us discuss them.

For taking notes:

Do Not Use Express Settings

When you're installing Windows 10 on your PC, you'll be asked to choose between **Custom** or **Express Settings** during the setup. Don't make the mistake of selecting Express Settings.

Not that the Express Settings is bad but it doesn't let you take full control of your privacy. But if you select Custom, you are able to take full charge of your privacy from when you're Windows is set off. You be able to edit the Settings that manages your private data.

Ad Tracking

If you didn't heed my word and you still decided to use Express Settings, it's a given that The OS will monitor any of your activity and information.

And then it gathers this information it has gotten and supplies them to its Ad associates which in turn uses this to shoot ads at you. And not only online, also in Windows.

IF ad tracking is enabled on you Windows 10, Windows produces what they a call an advertising ID for you. Applications can then get their hands on the ID and use to supply ads they think you'll be interested in according to your information.

To turn this bad boy off, (because let's get real not all of us like to be bothered by ads)
1. Select the Windows start at the lower left of the screen
2. Click the **Settings**, that's the gear symbol
3. Choose the **Privacy** icon
4. Select **General**
5. Look for **Let apps use advertising ID to make**....... And toggle it off.

Camera Control

I always have this feeling that someone is always watching, not through CCTV or DSLR but from the camera on my PC.

Some solve this issue the 'Actionable way' and paste tape over the camera. But you don't have to do that (not saying you shouldn't) But there's another more modern and efficient way

1. Click the Start at the left corner
2. Click the **Setting** gear
3. Choose **Camera**
4. Toggle off **Let apps use my camera**
5. Or you can leave it on and specify which apps can access the camera

But note that this method only block off apps from getting into the camera hardware. But Windows can still use it's built in Windows camera to capture photos and record videos. But it will only do so when you tell it to

If your mind is still not at rest, hey just put the tape.

Location Tracking

If you loved the sound of that, then maybe you don't need to turn of this setting. But for anyone like me, that just sounds a lot creepy. Because with this, Windows apps are able to find out the location of your computer. Not just your general location like 'Hey, he lives in Europe' But your exact specific location.

Not that you're a scam or anything but you never know whos tracking you from the web and use this info to barge into your house

To disable
1. Select the Start
2. Hit the **Settings**
3. Then **Privacy**
4. Select **Location**
5. Toggle off **Location**

IN Location history below, click clear to erase any history that Windows has of your location

Chapter 8

Networking Basics

This chapter is a critical one. Your windows 10 operating system must explore the internet, except you don't give a damn about the internet; like my aged uncle, Thomas. Understanding the networking basics of Windows 10 will help you take charge of your internet access without having a lot of issues.

For taking notes:

Client and Server

One vital connection on network is the relationship of the client and the server. When we talk about server, we are talking of a computer in which media files, websites, chat apps are stored. On example of a server is the computer where the www.google.com (the search page for Google) is stored

A client on the other hand is another computer that requests or seeks to use or download content. This computer doesn't have to be a literal computer, it can be your smartphone, tablet or PC. So when you search out www.google.com on your phone and it connects through a network, your phone is a client.

IP Addresses

Computers need to find out origins and destinations to send data through a network. So the way the computer identifies it is through Internet Protocol addresses (IP)s. IP addresses are group of four numbers . These numbers ranges from 1 to 254. Example; 153.173.45.8.

There are types of IP addresses. We have Public IP address. These are available and reachable wherever on the internet. But with the other; Private IP, they aren't accessible anyplace. Many of them are hidden behind some computer that has a Public IP address.

Switches and Hubs

Computers are customarily connected together through cables. This then creates a network. Ethernet is the cable that is used mostly, and it contains 4 pairs of wires that are in a plastic covering. But since cables alone don't really create a nice network, we began to use a network hub.

A hub is just like an outlet where different computer are plugged into with a Ethernet cable. So if all computer are plugged to a hub and one wants to send information to another, it just sends it to the hub which in turn send it to the other computers.

When using a hub to send messages to different computers at the same time, it can puzzle the hub and slow down the network. So networks began using a switch. What a switch does is that it sends message to the destination is was intended to alone. When using a switch, a computer can send message to only one other computer that it wants to send to without the other computers receiving it. The others can still send message to each other without meddling

Routers

With all the messages that go through the network, Routers decides whether to pass these messages **to** the outside networks or **from** the outside networks.

Routers do three main things,

1. **Separate**: They separate networks into different sections or the bond networks together

2. **Allocate IP addresses**: Routers give IP addresses using Dynamic Host Configuration Protocol or DHCP

3. **Protect**: Routers also protect the private networks and keep users out of them. With the Firewall built in some routers, they are able to shut out unwanted messages so they don't get to computers

Chapter 9

Basic Troubleshooting

Aha! This is perhaps one part of the book you're likely gonna be interested in. You see, like every other operating system, Windows 10 basic troubleshooting guides to help you with minor glitches.

For taking notes:

When a program is slow

If a program doesn't work right or is going slow, you can
1. Close the program and open it again
2. Or Shutdown your PC and after few seconds has passed turn it on again. Some problems should disappear with this step
3. Find out from the company if there's any software update or any problems relating to the one you have

When A Program Doesn't Respond At All

When a program doesn't respond, you can
1. Press **Ctrl**, **Alt** and **Delete** and hold. This should open up the Task Manger. Select the program that's being stubborn and Hit End Task

Network Problems

1. Restart your PC. Restarting your computer is like the first thing you should think of when your computer faces problems and it can help fix your network problems

2. Doing a quick reset of the network hardware can also help.
   - Remove the power from your modem and router. Wait for about 35 seconds and plug back the power for the modem
   - Wait for about a minute for the modem to finish powering
   - After the modem has connected, put back the power for the router. And after the router powers you should be able to use the network

3. If you stay in a crowded place where they are many Wi-Fi networks, this can cause a lot interference and connection problems. Try changing the channel of your wireless network

4. There might be a problem with your DNS cache. So if some pages don't load, you can flush the DNS cache.

5. If you've tried everything, try letting your internet service provider know abou the problem

The 'Shutting Down' Won't Go

Sometimes the shutdown message doesn't go away and it just stays there and computer doesn't shut down.

1. Long press the power button of the computer for about ten seconds till the computer goes off.

Sound Doesn't Come On

1. Check the taskbar to find the volume control and increase it. Or go to Control Panel
2. If you're using Windows Media Player or any other media player, check and increase the volume
3. If using external speakers, be sure that they are on
4. Try using headphones to determine if the problem is from the computer itself

Computer Makes Noise

1. One of the main causes of the computer making noise is because if the accumulated dust in it. Tyr cleaning the computer. It is said that the inside of the computer should be cleaned every 6 months

2. Try changing the fan or cooler inside your computer

Chapter 10

Windows 10 Tips And Tricks

This chapter discuses basic Windows 10 tricks that can help new users master the operating system within a short while.

For taking notes:

Making Calls with Skype

To make a call with Skype on your windows 10,
1. Open up **Phonebook**
2. Select the persons contact name
3. A profile should open up, Depending on the one you wish to use, select either phone call or video call

And just in case you've called the person before, you can still see their names in the video call history. When you go to the call history, you select their name and it should start calling

Receiving Calls on Skype

If someone calls you on your computer, you will see an alert show up on you display. Then you;

1. Click an anyplace in the area of the picture to answer the call
2. Click **ignore** if you would like to reject the call

If you would like to answer with only audio or answer with just a message and not use video or audio, click options and choose among the list provided.

Using the Mail App on Your Windows 10

In the Windows 10 with the mail app, you can add different accounts, yahoo, outlook, Gmail and begin to send and receive email.

1. Enter the **Mail app**
2. If you've not used the Mail app before, you'll be asked to add an account
3. If this is not the first time you're using the Mail app, Click **Settings** then **Mange Accounts** and choose the kind of account you want to use
4. Input your email and password

To send an email
1. Open the **Mail app** on your computer
2. Choose the account that you wish to use
3. When that opens, Click **New Mail**
4. Input the email address of the person you want to send an email to in the **To** area
5. Select the message body so you can start to type in your message

Editing Your Photos in Windows 10

With the photos app in Windows 10, the ordinary person does not need super editing programs. We don't do too much editing, just the basics. And the photos app can help you do just that. You can crop, resize, or retouch your photos.

Trust me, you'll be glad you upgraded from windows 7. To edit a photo,

1. Enter the **Photos app**.
2. Select the photo
3. Click on the pencil symbol so you can enter the editing kingdom
4. Now you have an array of options you can use to edit.

Don't do overboard though with the editing, just do it slightly.

Importing Photos in Windows 10

To import images using the **Photos App**
1. Select **Start**
2. Then **All Photos**
3. Click **Photos**
4. Make sure you've connected the device you want to import from, and select import at the top bar
5. Choose the photos you want to import
6. Hit **Continue**

The Start Menu

You may be the type that likes the old start menu. The start menu where the options are listed and not tiled, you still have the opportunity to have it.

1. Check for the windows icon at the bottom corner of the screen at the left.
2. Right click it
3. A list of should appear and you will see different options like **Mobility center** or the **Apps and Features**.

It the standard view, you can access these options. But I think it's more quicker this way

Just Shake

There's this cool feature in the windows 10 that many don't know of. When your screen if cramped with many windows, you can easily clear it by holding the top of the window you want to remain and you just wiggle or shake it. This will minimize the remaining windows

If you want to bring back the minimized windows, you can just shake again and they will return to the screen

Flip The Display

If it just so happens that you want to rotate your screen, you can do so by just clicking **Ctrl + Alt + D** at the same time with any arrow key you want.

If you choose the down arrow, it will rotate it upside down. If you select the left or right keys, those will flip it 90 degrees. If you select the upward arrow key, it will bring it back to the standard view. This option will be really helpful if you use several displays

Or you can just
1. Go to **Graphics Options**
2. Then **Rotation**

Form here you'll be able to rotate the view to any way you deem best

Reveal the Desktop Button

If you check the right corner of the display at the bottom, you'll find the mystery button. There's a probability that you might not have found it yet. Look closely at the corner, past the time and you will see something like a silver of a button.

If you don't see it, drag your cursor to the very corner. You click it and it will minimize all the windows that are open. This is really great if you want to view the desktop really quick.

You can also make it possible that this feature will minimize open windows when you just hover on the button. To enable this,
1. Go to **Settings**
2. Chose **Personalization**
3. Then **Taskbar**
4. Toggle on **Use Peek To View Desktop When You Move Your Mouse To**

Access Other Features

There's one cool feature that enables you be able to access very quickly many toolbar presets like Window schemes, enter the task manger or Cortana the Microsoft assistant

There are other options you can choose from. What are you waiting for, just right click the taskbar already to access this option.

Open taskbar apps in a flash

This one is more than a lifesaver. It has been there all along and we didn't know. This is a method for you to open the items on your task as fast as possible. If you check your taskbar at the bottom, you'll see a row of apps that has been pinned there. It might be File explorer or Chrome, you'll most likely have an app or apps pinned to the taskbar

To open the apps there quickly, press and hold the **Window key** on your keyboard and press the number that fits to its location on the taskbar.

For example if Chrome is the second app on the taskbar, all you have to do is long press the **Windows key** and press 2 and it will open up in a flash.

Look for the slow apps

This reminds me of those frustrating times when the computer starts dragging and becoming slow. The only thing one can do is to hold his breath as the computer drags and wastes time. That should not be the case anymore, you should go and fetch out the app in your computer that's slowing it down.

1. Enter the **Task manager**
2. Go to **Processes**
3. You will now be shown the apps that are running and how much space each one of them is using

Open up the Task manager

Since we are still on task manager, why don't we talk about a way to call it up rather quickly? You can do it by right-clicking on the Start. Or you want it the keyboard way, click **Ctrl + Alt + Delete** simultaneously and choose it from the option that shows up.

The task manger was actually just a simple feature that you basically use to close the programs that prove to be unresponsive. But with your windows 10, the Task Manager is a lot more.

Sharing files

You will want to send or transfer files or documents to your family members or they might want to send to you, sure you can do it through email but you can do it the better way. You can put everyone in the family on a Windows network. This will enable you to share files.

1. Press the **Start icon**. It's at the lower left corner of the display
2. Next you enter **Settings**, it's the gear symbol
3. Then **Network & Internet**
4. Select **home group**
5. Choose **Create home group**

Use the task scheduler

Using the task scheduler on your computer can be really helpful. And as the name implies, it schedules task that you set. Like for example, it can turn off the computer when you set for at a certain time.

To access the task scheduler, just type out Task Scheduler in your taskbar and start using it.

Open apps easily

If you open up the start, you should see a set of apps that show on the side. The apps that you use most will be listed at the top while the remaining apps are just shown in A-Z order.

If you scroll through, you will find the one that you wish to open up. But you don't have to go skimming through all of them. You can just click a letter. This will then open the whole letters. Type the first letter of the program or the app you wish to open. Then you be directed to it

Drag windows to a corner

This feature is accessible on the Windows 10. Click on any window and move it to the side. This should now fit it to half of the display.

You can also click it and drag it to any corner of the screen you want so that the window will then fit about a quarter of the screen. Just in case you're making use of multiple screens. Move it to a border corner and a prompt should show up to notify you if you would like to open or move the app to the corner of the display

You can also invoke something like this when you use the **Windows key** together with any of the **arrow keys** for a quicker method.

Make the command prompt almost invisible

If you're the type that like to get your hands busy in the inward parts on windows through the command prompts, windows 10 offers you a way to make the Command Prompt go transparent mode

To reach the command prompt, select the windows and type in the word Command Prompt and click it. This will make you access the app quickly.

To customize the view,
1. Right-click the top of the window.
2. Select **Properties** from the prompt it brings
3. Go to **colors**
4. Look below to find the slider for opacity, slide it down to make the command prompt transparent

This will go a long way as it will enable you to use the Command Prompt and still see through it to do other things

Speech typing

Yeah you read right, I said speech typing. With Windows 10, Microsoft made speech recognition really easy to use and it can get addictive very fast

1. Move over to **Settings**
2. Select **Privacy**
3. Then **Speech**
4. Switch on the toggle

From here onwards, you can make use of **Windows key** and **H** if you are in a text area to bring up Cortana to record your voice. It does so by means of the windows microphone and it then writes out your sayings in the text area. Though you have to say punctuations manually, like saying comma or full stop. But it think it's a cool feature to try out.

Enable file explorer in dark mode

You can use the dark mode for the taskbar or even the Start menu before. But now you have an edge with the windows 10 to be able to use it in **File explorer**

To setup the dark mode,
1. Go to **Settings**
2. Then **Personalization**
3. Select **colors**
4. Move to the bottom where you'll find the option to switch to dark.

Use focus assist to quiet notifications

This option was known as Quiet hours before. But in the revamped 2018 update, you have more control on the notifications that show on your computer.

1. Go to **Settings**
2. Then **System**
3. Select **Focus assist**

You can choose Priority only to select specific contacts.

Chapter 11

Using Cortana

Cortana, Microsoft's voice assistant, has always been fun. If you have been a fan of Microsoft Windows, you'll enjoy using Cortana. And with Windows 10 finally hitting the shelves, Cortana has grown better than ever. Sometimes, I feel it's even better than Siri. When Microsoft first released the voice assistant, it was meant for the Windows phone 7. Yes, it was a mobile app. In time, the wonderful app called Cortana stretched its wings into becoming compatible with desktop computers, laptops, tablets and anything that runs Windows 10. Good news, you'll agree.

You may have heard that Microsoft is going to replace Internet Explorer with a new browser called Edge. Cortana and Edge are designed to work together. The voice assistant pops up in the address bar and waits for you to ask about something.

When you highlight a particular word or phrase and right-click it, Cortana will summon a sidebar with a definition and related links to help you dive deeper. This is especially useful if there's a subject you want to researvh, a word you don't understand, or a question about related terms.

Also, you can ask the voice assistant for some help locating a document, and she can search across available data, both on your hard drive and in the cloud. Professionals or students who may keep a large amount of documents and collaborative projects on OneDrive or in other places, will find this helpful.

Cortana has already, a built-in attitude. She can make a joke, sing a quick song, make fun of Siri, and even deride past Microsoft fumbles like Clippy. Also, you can ask her for opinions about previous Microsoft leaders.

In summary, Cortana will help you easily undertake certain tasks, like tracking your packages automatically, providing you with accurate weather information, and ensuring you don't miss any important appointments.

Using Cortana isn't any difficult. I am going to explain, with steps, how to explore Cortana. The following subheading will discuss impressive Cortana tips and tricks.

TRACKING PACKAGES WITH CORTANA

Tracking packages automatically with Cortana might be difficult, but you can add a tracking ID manually so Cortana can keep an eye on your package from supported carriers, including FedEx, UPS, and DHL, and from supported retailers, like Microsoft store, Amazon.com, eBay, Target, Apple, and Wal-Mart.

For you to quickly start tracking a package, do the following:

1. Use the Windows key + S to open Cortana.
2. Type in the tracking ID of the package.
3. Once Cortana validates the information, click Track your package.

Alternatively, a more accurate way to track a package is using the following steps:

1. Use the Windows key + S to open Cortana.
2. Click on the **Notebook** button in the navigation pane.

3. Scroll down and click **Packages**.
4. Ensure that Package tracking cards option is turned on.
5. Click **Add a package** and enter the tracking information. Then click the result to add the ID properly.
6. Click on Save to complete.

Once the information is in the Notebook, each time you open Cortana, you will see a card showing the latest status of the package.

USING CORTANA FOR TECHNICAL SUPPORT

For newbies, Cortana can also offer entry-level technical support. Simply ask questions like the examples below:

- How do I install a printer?
- How do I project my screen?
- How do I change my background?
- How do I change default apps?
- How do I update Windows?
- How do I make a backup?

Most of the answers will be converted into Bing search queries or you will be directed to a Microsoft support page. For further directions, there are instructions right in the Cortana app.

USING CORTANA AS YOUR PERSONAL TRANSLATOR

There is no need to open your web browser and use an online translator. Cortana is able to translate a wide variety of languages right from the search box -- where available, you also get a play button to read aloud the translation.

To use the translation feature, do the following:

1. open Cortana and type "translate" followed by the word or phrase and the name of the language you want the content translated.
2. Hit Enter.

You have two options. You either hit **Translate Hello to Spanish,** or you say, **Hey Cortana: How do I say Hello in French.**

Cortana can currently translate in the following languages: Bosnian, Bulgarian, Catalan, Chinese (Simplified), Chinese (Traditional), Croatian, Czech, Danish, Dutch, English, Estonian, Finnish, French, German, Greek, Haitian Creole, Hebrew, Hindi, Hmong Daw, Hungarian, Indonesian, Italian, Japanese, Kiswahili, Klingon, Klingon (plqaD), Korean, Latvian, Lithuanian, Malay,

Maltese, Norwegian, Persian, Polish, Portuguese, Querétaro Otomi, Romanian, Russian, Serbian (Cyrillic), Serbian (Latin), Slovak, Slovenian, Spanish, Swedish, Thai, Turkish, Ukrainian, Urdu, Vietnamese, and Welsh.

USING CORTANA TO CREATE LOCATION-BASED REMINDERS

Cortana can track and remind you of important events, and since the assistant works across devices, you can set it to remind you to do something at certain locations on your PC and get reminded on your phone. For example, you can say **Hey Cortana: Next time I'm at the mall, remind me to buy a new shoe.**

When you are at that particular location, Cortana will pop in your phone the reminder to get a new shoe, even though it is on your PC that you have created the reminder.

SENDING AN SMS FROM YOUR PC WITH CORTANA

You can send a message using Cortana. This depends on the information you have in your contact list. If the recipient's phone number isn't in the contact list, you'll need to open the **People**

app and update their phone number information before sending the message.

You can simply say: **Hey Cortana: Send text and follow the on-screen instructions.**

When you hit the Send button, Cortana will sync the text to your phone. Then it will send it through your phone to the recipient.

IMPROVING CORTANA VOICE RECOGNITION

This tip will be useful to you if you're not a native speaker of the language setup on Windows 10. Cortana may find it hard trying to understand you. Sometimes, the assistant may not even respond to the common "Hey Cortana" voice command.

To improve Cortana voice recognition there are two things you can do:

First, you can adjust Windows 10 speech settings to help Cortana recognize non-native accents.

Second, you can change the settings to let the assistant answer only to you, thus letting it learn your voice.

After changing these settings, Cortana will be able to answer more accurately to your voice commands and better understand your accent.

CORTANA KEYBOARD SHORTCUTS

Microsoft has included a few keyboard shortcuts to interact with Cortana. They include:

1. Windows key + C keyboard shortcut to open Cortana in listening mode.
2. Windows key + S keyboard shortcut to open Cortana home screen directly into typing search mode. Or, you can also use the * *Windows key + Q** keyboard shortcut.

So far, we have seen that Windows 10 is an operating system with impressive tools. Beginners and seniors who which to learn more about using Windows 10 can do so with constant practice. The age-old adage that says, practice makes perfect, still olds water today. As you use your system, you'll discover ideas that will make you a pro sooner than you had ever thought.

Chapter 12

Windows 10 Shortcuts

Using shortcuts on the Windows 10 is a very fast way for you to increase your productivity when you work.

Here, well discuss the top Windows 10 shortcuts that will get you to switch between Windows, split the screens, do some multitasking in desktop and others.

When you want to learn the keyboard shortcuts, you could say it's like learning a new language. And just like learning a language, you don't get it all at first.

You'll start small as you build up your vocabulary. In time you'll get to understand and speak the language well.

So it is with the shortcuts for your Windows 10, you want to begin building your vocabulary with the things that you do regularly like switching from one program to another. When you do it'll stick to your memory and you'll remember.

Some of the things that you can learn first is minimizing Windows, looking for programs, multitasking through files, getting along with Windows search and finding some documents and files.

When you start to learn your short cuts with the things that you make use of regularly like these, you'll build your confidence with shortcut, speed up the activities that you carry out in Windows 10 and you'll get motivated to learn more since you're already seeing success with the small tasks.

Windows key + 1 or another number

Take a look at the taskbar, what you'll see is a row of applications and programs lined up. If you have an app that you make use of more than others, you can just add it to the row. In fact you could add it to the first place.

So let's say that **Google Chrome** is as the first app on your taskbar, you can just press **Windows key + 1** to get it open. You can also try this too with other apps. Like if an app is in the 3rd position, you can just use **Windows key + 3** to open it up.

If you would like to add your favourite app to the taskbar, follow these steps

1. Press the **Win** key and enter in the name of the app
2. Right-click the app

3. Choose the option for **Pin to taskbar**

4. The app will now be in the taskbar. You can also click and drag it to any position you want to on the taskbar

So you can add any program (except the File Explorer) to the taskbar and move it to any position you want. The reason you done want to add the File Explorer is because it already has its own shortcut. More on that in a bit

Windows key + left

There are variations to this command, you can also try **Windows key + right, Windows key + up** and **Windows key + down.**

What they all do is that they send the window or program that is currently open to the side of the screen. The left and right commands will send it to the left and right of the screen while the up and down commands will send the window reduce the size to the top and bottom of the screen.

If you have 2 apps open and you click **Windows key + left** or **Windows key + right** for a particular app, you'll be asked to set the other app to fill the empty area of the screen.

Windows key then type or Ctrl + E then type

The search option that exists in Windows is like the best thing ever. It definitely gets top rank in the list of useful. The reason for this is that you can basically find anything through it.

With this option, you don't have to fiddle around trying to find a particular file or app. You just use the search.

All you do is press the **Win key** and input the name of the program of app that you're looking for and tada!! It'll show up. It has no excuse not to.

In fact, you don't have to include the full name of the program before Windows brings it out to you. I'm looking for **Google Chrome** and all it did was type in '**Go**' and it supplies it at the top of the list.

Alt + F

This is a cool way to enter the file menu options in a program. Like for example in Microsoft word, where you have the **File, Home, Insert** and others. The **Alt + F** option will enable you to open the file menu.

It is kind of a stress to scroll all the way to the top just to reach the file option.

And it's not only the file you can reach with a shortcut.

When you press the **Alt** key, you'll see the key that you need to press to get the other options to show. Still in Microsoft word and you press the **Alt** key. It will you that **Alt + H** will enter the **Home** and **Alt + N** will open **Insert**.

Ctrl + Shift + Esc

This will get you to open the task manager quickly. You can also try to enter the search and type in '**Task Manager**'. But the **Ctrl + Shift + Esc** option is quicker.

Alt + Enter

When you select a file or a document and you want to see the properties, you don't have to right click and choose **Properties**. You can just easily press **Alt + Enter** and the properties window will open up.

It's in this properties segment that you'll be able to see the size of the file, the date when it was created, date it was modified and other properties of the file.

Another shortcut to summon the properties window is to use **Alt + right click**. It does the same thing; bring up the properties menu.

Windows key + E

When it comes to looking for apps and programs, the best place to turn to is the Windows search. But when it comes to looking files and documents, the File Explorer is great at it.

The reason for this is not only because the name says 'File' Explorer but also because it does some filtering features that allow users to be able to narrow down what they search for. This method is an efficient way to dig through and find files in your computer.

For you to summon the File Explorer in shortcut style, you just use **Windows key + E**. Now you'll see a wide array of options that you use to search for your file. You'll see navigational options, filers and views that you can use to improve your 'search experience'

In the search bar at the top right, you can input the name of a file you want to find. But something else that you can try to do again is to input the extension. Like you add the .jpg or .png if you are looking for a photo. Or, you can find a document with the .docx extension

Windows key + Ctrl + D

This button will help you to create another desktop. And by another desktop it's a virtual one.

Windows key + Ctrl + left or right

This will help to go scroll through the desktops. Pressing the left key will return to the previous desktops you were in.

Pressing the right key will scroll you through the newer desktops you just created.

Windows key + Ctrl + F4

So you're done with the virtual desktop, you want to close it, and you have no idea how. You just have to press **Windows key + Ctrl + F4** to quit it. Just make sure that you saved all you were doing on the new desktop.

Ctrl + E

Lovely way to turn on the search. You can make use of this option in the File Explorer. This will help you to search the current folder you are in.

When you hit the Ctrl + E option on your keyboard, the cursor will jump to the search box at the right hand corner of the screen. So you have a fast way to search for a file. Just press **Windows key + E** to enter File Explorer and **Ctrl + E** to search for the item.

This doesn't only work in File Explorer. It will also work when you are in a web browser (or at least for most modern browser). Try it for Microsoft Edge or Google Chrome. Pressing the **Ctrl + E** will send you to the address bar for you to enter the any URL.

Windows key + X

This option will get you to open up the start menu options. Normally you would have to right click the **Start** to show up this menu.

This is the menu that houses the mobility center, program and features, device manager, task manager and more.

Windows key + I

This is a quick way to launch the **Settings** window. If you are looking for a particular setting, you can use to the search to find it.

Alt + Tab

Another option that makes the list among the cool is the **Alt + Tab** function. What this does is it makes to be able to switch between Windows very quickly.

Let's say that you are working on Microsoft Word and Google Chrome. Normally, you'll have to go to the bottom of the taskbar to select the program you want to switch to or you can just minimize the current program you're in to get to the other one.

But with the **Alt + Tab** option you can switch easily. You can press the combo once and then you'll go to the other program that's opened.

You can also press it again to switch back to the previous window. That's for 2 programs. What happens when there are 3 or more programs opened?

Easy enough. When there are multiple programs opened, pressing the **Alt + E** option won't get you to switch between all of them. All you have to do is to hold down the **Alt** button and then press the **Tab** continuously till it navigates to your desired window.

As you press the **Tab**. Don't release the **Alt** key.

Ctrl + Alt + Tab

This one is just like the option we just talked about. Except, you won't have to hold down the **Alt + key**. When you press this combo, all the windows will be opened to you just like the **Alt** key will do but this time it will remain like that.

This is the Tab Switch Freeze. Instead of letting you to just jump between windows and programs you just opened recently, you'll be able to see all the items that you've opened on your computer.

Then you can then switch to the one you would like to open. You can make use of the same **Tab** key or you just use the left and right controls to navigate through the windows

Windows key + R

This will have you opening up the **Run** dialog box

Windows key + A

When you get notifications they show up at the edge of your screen for a few seconds. You have those few seconds to select it and attend to the matter. If you wait any longer, it will disappear.

But you can still access the notification by going to the **Action Center**. Normally you have to go the corner of the display to access it. It is the icon that's just before the Date and Time. Yes, that one.

But the problem with that is it's too far. With **Windows key + A**, you'll get to it much faster. Just press it once and the Action Center opens up

Windows key + T

This is another method of switching through Windows. When you press the **Windows key + T**. you'll move through the options in the taskbar.

As you press **T** continuously, you'll see the taskbar run through the items on it. When it eventually gets to the app you want just hit **Enter** to open it up.

Alt + left or right

If you've opened many folders in File Explorer and you want to go back, this is a great option. Just hold the **Alt + left** and press left to go back.

You can press the **Alt + right** to return to the folder you just closed.

You should know that this shortcut will only get you to move through the folders that you've opened before. That is your search history. They will not get you to folders unless you have actually opened the folder before.

If you want to move a folder hierarchy. (That is the folder that houses the current folder you are in) you can just use **Alt + up**.

This shortcut does not just work for File Explorer only. The **Alt + right** and **Alt + left** shortcut can also work when you in a web browser. You'll be able to move forwards and backwards through the history of what you've searched for in the same tab.

No more looking for the back button on the screen, **Alt + left** does the trick. This works for most browsers like Chrome, Edge and Firefox.

Windows key + ,

It just gets better. If you would like to see the desktop and not minimize your apps this is the way to go

Pressing Windows key + , will get you to see the desktop briefly and return to your program. The longer you hold Windows key the longer the desktop stays.

Right-click taskbar + D

This is a good option to see what's going on in the computer if you opened different programs. All you have to do is just Right-click the taskbar at the bottom of screen and then press D

When you do this all the opened windows will be in cascade. That is will be stocked behind each other. When you use this cascade formation, you'll be able to find the apps that are open. If there's a program you don't want to use again, you can close it.

Right-click taskbar + U.

So you just tried the shortcut to cascade the windows. It worked, the windows are stacked behind each other now you want to get out of the mode.

You easily opt-out of the cascade option for the windows by Right-clicking on the taskbar then pressing U. this will revert the windows to the normal view and undo the cascade effect.

Before you actually do the 'uncascade' windows option, you should have used the cascade option first.

Right-click taskbar + E

The cascading option is great to see which programs are open on your computer. But there's a better way. It is the option to show windows stacked side-by-side. This does what it says. Its stacks the windows that are open.

All you have to do is Right-click the taskbar then press E. The way in which the windows will be stacked on your computer will depend on the number of apps or programs that you have opened and the type of documents and files that you have opened.

The windows will not be snapped to the corners, they'll just be resized and stacked. If you stacked the windows, and it has already served its purpose, you can always revert it back to the window you were in by Right-clicking the taskbar then pressing U.

Ctrl + F6

So let's say that you have two documents opened in Microsoft word. The normal way that you switch between them is by moving to the taskbar at the bottom, click the app icon then choose the document to enter.

Nice way. But too slow and it does reduce productivity. A quicker way; **Ctrl + F6**. This is the cycle program shortcut that will switch to the files that you opened for the same program.

If you opened, say 9 documents in Microsoft word, you can just press the **Ctrl + F6** and it will switch to the next document. Don't release the Ctrl and keep pressing F6. You'll see that it just keeps cycling through the files you opened.

Windows key + PrtSc

If you want to take screenshot on your computer, you can just press the PrtSc button on the keyboard. But that won't save it to the computer

Press **Windows key + PrtSc** and you'll be able to view the screenshot page in the pictures folder

Ctrl + M

Another option that you want to make use of to minimize all windows is the **Ctrl + M** shortcut. When you have many windows open, minimizing them one after the other with the minimize button at the top can be stressful

Especially when you have about 10 windows opened at once. **Ctrl + M** minimizes them all at once.

Ctrl + W

As you work with many files that are open in Windows 10, you may want to close out of a document but don't want to close out of the program itself. That was what this shortcut was made.

When you hit **Ctrl + W**, the current files that you make use of will be closed but the app will still be open.

What this means is if you hit **Ctrl + W** on a word document, the current files will be closed but Microsoft word itself will still be opened. You can then open another file. You will also be given to option to choose Save or Don't Save

You also make use of this **Ctrl + W** shortcut when you're in the multitasking view. You'll be able to use it to close any files that is opened at that moment.

Alt + F4

This shortcut should not be mistaken for **Ctrl + W**. The **Alt + F4** shortcut will not only quit the current file that you are working on but it will close you out of the application itself. When you press it, you'll also be given the option for Save or Don't Save.

When you press the **Alt + F4** on a word document, Windows will close any word document that is opened and also close Microsoft word. This very different from the **Ctrl + W** that only closes you out of the current file that is opened.

But that's not the only thing **Alt + F4** does. If you are on your windows desktop and you press the **Alt + F4** shortcut, you'll get the option to shut down your computer

If you are working on a file and you want to shutdown very quickly, you can just press **Ctrl + M** to minimize all the windows that are open then press **Alt + F4** to shut down your computer

Alt + Shift + D

This is a great way to insert the date very quickly. Pressing **Alt + Shift + D** will paste the date in format set is in your computer. **Alt + Shift + T** will get to paste the current time where the cursor is in a document.

Ctrl + N

When you're in Microsoft office suite, your go-to option for creating a new document should be the **Ctrl + N** shortcut. You can create new blank files very quickly and easily.

So if you working on Microsoft PowerPoint and you hit the **Ctrl + N**, a new presentation that you can work with will be opened to you.

Ctrl + N is also be very useful when you're managing your files with the Windows File Explorer. When you press the combo from File Explorer, you'll be given a new window that you can work with. Now you have 2 windows for the File Explorer. Snap it to split screen and you'll be able to drag and drop files into different folders.

If you created a window by opening Windows File Explorer afresh, you'll be shown the homepage. But by using Ctrl + N, you'll be given a replica of the folder you're in but in a different window.

Ctrl + Shift + N

Still on File Explorer hacks. If you are in a folder and you want to create a new folder, you just have to hit **Ctrl + Shift + N** and a new blank folder will be created.

With this method you can easily create folders on the fly without stress. You'll be able to organize files quicker leading to better productivity.

Normally you will have to right click an empty space in the file explorer, chose New, then select folder. That method is long and stressful. It even makes one reconsider creating a new folder when one thinks of the process he has to go through.

But now, Ctrl + Shift + N makes it ever easier

Ctrl + Shift + >

This is a quick way to increase the size of a text. Instead of moving all the way up simply pressing **Ctrl + Shift + >** will do the trick

Ctrl + Shift + <

With **Ctrl + Shift + >**, you'll be able to decrease the size of the selected text. To decrease the size even further, keep pressing the > while the Ctrl + Shift is still held down

Right click + W + document

Creating a new folder with **Ctrl + Shift + N** is a fast and easy way to create empty folders. But what if you want to create new file without entering the program.

Yes it is possible to create a new document and not get into the application itself. You can do this for any Microsoft office application.

If you want to create a new blank document of an application, you just have to

1. Right click an area in the folder you want to the document to be ·
2. Press **W** to get to the New option
3. Choose the type of file you want to open

When you choose the file type, you'll see a new document of the application will be created. It will have the default name so you may have to enter a new one.

The file is created. And you did all this without having to open the application itself.

Windows key + +

Have you been finding yourself squinting to find out what is written on the screen of your computer? You may enlarged the text size for the application but maybe that's not enough or you don't want it zoomed in permanently.

Your next option is to use the **Windows key + +** shortcut. When you press the combo, you'll see the items on your screen become magnified. That's because you just opened the magnifier.

If you want to get a more zoomed in view you keep pressing the +. Just make sure that you don't release the Windows key.

Windows key + -

This does the same as the previous shortcut; magnifier. Except this one does the opposite; it zooms out. The zooming out does not happen when you're in the normal view of the screen.

There nothing to zoom out from at that point. But when you use the **Windows key + +** shortcut, you can easily use the **Windows key + +** shortcut to reverse the effect.

Ctrl + End

If you are using Microsoft word or any other word editing program, one easy way to go the end of the is to use Ctrl + End. The normal way to do it is by using the slider at the right side of the page.

Then you drag it to the end, but that's okay. But why would you use that when you've got **Ctrl + End**

Ctrl + Home

The opposite of the last option. You'll be able to use the **Ctrl + Home** shortcut to move directly to the beginning of the document.

Shift + Home

When you want to highlight a document in word, the normal procedure is to click and drag to the end of the word.

Not only is that method slow when it comes to highlighting all the texts in the same line, but you can select something else. The **Shift + Home** shortcut makes it easier

When you use the shortcut, the word from the cursor to the beginning of the line will be selected.

Shift + End.

This does the opposite of the previous shortcut. **Shift + End** will highlight from the end of the text to where the cursor is.

Disclaimer

In as much as the author believes beginners will find this book helpful in learning how to use a Windows 10 operating device, it is only a small book. It should not be relied upon solely for all Windows 10 tricks and troubleshooting.

About the author

Stephen Rock has been a certified apps developer and tech researcher for more than 12 years. Some of his 'how to' guides have appeared in a handful of international journals and tech blogs. He loves rabbits.

Facebook page @ Newcomers Guide

Also by the Author

1. IPHONE USER MANUAL FOR NEWCOMERS: All in one iOS 12 guide for beginners and seniors (iPhone, 8, X, XS & XS Max user guide)\
2. APPLE WATCH USER GUIDE FOR NEWCOMERS: The unofficial Apple Watch series 4 user manual for beginners and seniors
3. 3D PRINTING GUIDE FOR NEWCOMERS
4. SAMSUNG GALAXY S9 PLUS USER MANUAL FOR NEWCOMERS

For taking notes:

www.ingramcontent.com/pod-product-compliance
Lightning Source LLC
Chambersburg PA
CBHW031242050326
40690CB00007B/913